Praise for Re...

In this poignant volume, Shelley Brandon presents a series of stories that invite, even dare us to see and to appreciate the rich moments of shared humanity between young children and the adults who work alongside them every day.

For Brandon, heartbreak is a generative, fruitful occurrence rather than a destructive one. Each of Brandon's stories emphasizes the ways that, upon breaking, our hearts are suffused with new appreciations, wonderings, inspirations, and – always – a deep humility and reverence toward the work of not only teaching, but most importantly of living with children. I was instantly drawn into these intimate and vulnerable portraits of Shelley's days in the forest with her children, and inspired at every turn by the wonder and respect either which she regards each of them and the communities that they co-create.

On a more personal note, these stories make me long again for my own days wandering forest paths with young children. Each one is both paean and elegy to time that moves all too quickly and yet, inevitably, moves all the same. My heart is reminded of how valuable it is to be attentive to children, my heart is reminded to trust them and their abilities to know the world and others, and my heart is inspired to deeper love for the beautiful – indeed, heartbreaking – work.

—**Ron Grady,** Teacher-Researcher, Author and Illustrator of *What Does Brown Mean to You?*, and Author of *Honoring the Moment in Young Children's Lives*

What do we see breaking in these stories? Perhaps the thin veneer of professionalism that urges us to objectively assess skills and to be in control, is breaking open to allow for recognition of the interconnectedness of everything in our planet, and of children's whole-hearted embrace of these relationships. What good is a heart if it can't break out of this kind of prison?

Shelley Brandon's poetic narrative paints pictures of what it is to be deeply attuned to the vibrations all around us – to the sensibilities of all our relations. She is an educator who has reclaimed the privilege to be truly, aesthetically, present alongside whole-hearted toddlers. We are invited into the provocative refocusing that happens when one word is added – from "I felt my heart break", to "I felt my heart break open", and to recognize the values we can bring to our work with children that will welcome these kinds of liberating breaks.

Kintsugi is the name for Japanese pottery that highlights the beauty of breaks and cracks with gold. While kintsugi has endured and been admired for centuries, it is thought that its longevity may be due to its tender embrace of accidents and mistakes. Shelley recognizes how much we can learn from this kind of embrace, and helps us to reflect on the many heart-, spirit-, and mind-filling opportunities we may crush in well-intentioned efforts to prevent these cracks from happening. In these precious stories, she invites us to join in this life-enriching heartbreak.

—**Karyn Callaghan,**
President, Ontario Reggio Association

Reimagining Heartbreak weaves a charming spell. Shelley brings you down on the ground, into the woods, and into the preschoolers' world where heart-breaking experiences, both happy and sad, abound. The children find walking sticks, get stuck, cry, get amazed and Shelley allows her heart to break open and feel their joy and pain as her joy and pain. Literacy and numeracy are quietly absent. Early childhood education can be about opening up to happiness and sadness for the children and teachers alike. Shelley captivates us with these openings.

—**David Sobel,** Professor Emeritus, Antioch University and Author, *Wild Play: Parenting Adventures in the Great Outdoors, Childhood and Nature: Design Principles for Educators,* and *Place-Based Education: Connecting Classrooms and Communities*

reimagining heartbreak

an educator's journey to reclaim whole-heartedness

shelley brandon

edited by ann pelo and margie carter

Exchange Press

ISBN 978-0-942702-92-7
eISBN 978-0-942702-93-4

Printed in the United States.

© 2024 Shelley Brandon

Book Design: Stacy Hawthorne
Editors: Ann Pelo and Margie Carter
Managing Editor: Erin Glenn
Illustrations: Chad Hawthorne

This book may not be reproduced in whole or in part by any means without written permission of the publisher.

For more information about other
Exchange Press publications and resources
for directors and teachers, contact:

Exchange Press
7700 A Street
Lincoln, NE 68510
(800) 221-2864 • ExchangePress.com

A NOTE FROM THE EDITORS

A Call to Reimagine Our Work

The stories in the *Reimagining Our Work* (ROW) collection are anchored in the conviction that another world is possible for early childhood education – a world characterized by open-hearted and attentive collaborations between children and educators, in shared exploration of engaging ideas. This collection helps us begin to imagine that world, as we reimagine our work, moving beyond the joyless land of prescribed curricula with its corresponding outcomes and assessments, into the unpredictable, green-growing terrain of lively curiosity and rigorous critical thought.

Too often in our field, the discourse about educators reflects a diminished and disrespectful view of their capabilities for challenging, rigorous, generative thought. "Keep things simple and easily digestible," is a common caution. "Teachers want strategies that they can put immediately to use in their classrooms. Don't offer too much theory, too much complexity."

We disagree. **Strongly.** We believe that educators hunger for deeper meaning in their work. We believe that educators long to be challenged into their biggest, deepest, most startling thinking and questioning. We believe that educators are ready to have their hearts cracked open and their imaginations ignited. We believe that educators are eager to explore how theory looks in everyday practice and how practice can inform theory. These convictions are at the heart of this collection of stories.

In these stories, children and educators take up ideas of substance, pursuing questions in ways that are unscripted and original. They braid fluid imagination and expansive awareness into their collaborative inquiry. The children in these stories aren't "gifted" or privileged – except by the gift and privilege of their educators' potent regard for their capability, and their concomitant willingness to bring their best minds and hearts to the table.

Which is just what we see the educators do in these stories. We hear educators reflect – in their unique voices and contexts – on their evolving understandings of children's capacities, and their roles as educators, and the meaning and practice of teaching and learning. The educators in these stories hold assumptions and visions different from the dominant paradigm in our field, and we have much to learn from them.

With the ROW collection, we hope to advance the conversation among early childhood educators, administrators, community college and university educators, policy makers and funders about the nature and practice of early education – a conversation which we also engage in the foundational book for this collection,

From Teaching to Thinking: A Pedagogy for Reimagining Our Work. As you read, we hope that you are challenged, exhilarated, unsettled, and rejuvenated. We hope that you find kinship in these stories. We hope that the stories in this collection carry your thinking far beyond curriculum ideas, and help you reimagine your work. May these stories sustain you as you stand strong with the children in your care. Resist the limitations of standardized curriculum, and claim, instead, the exhilaration of creating a new world, together with children.

—Ann Pelo and *Margie Carter*
   Editors of the *Reimagining Our Work* (ROW) Collection

   Authors of *From Teaching to Thinking: A Pedagogy for Reimagining Our Work*

For more information on the
ROW collection and upcoming titles
please visit ExchangePress.com/ROW

contents

Foreword 13

Introduction 23

Chapter One: *The Forest as Home Ground* 37

Chapter Two: *The Teacher* 47

Chapter Three: *The Gift* 55

Chapter Four: *Stuck* 65

Chapter Five: *Snow Monkeys* 79

Chapter Six: *Snail Encounter* 87

Chapter Seven: *Broken* 97

Chapter Eight: *Hush* 107

About the Author 121

Coda 123

Study Guide 127

Colophon 136

foreword

"There is a crack, a crack in everything," Leonard Cohen sings in his "Anthem." "That's how the light gets in.[1]"

> *Ring the bells that still can ring*
> *Forget your perfect offering*
> *There is a crack, a crack in everything*
> *That's how the light gets in*

This could be the theme song for this book.

Shelley's stories about her forest explorations with toddlers ring with aching beauty, with marvel, but not because of any perfect offering. They ring with Shelley's presence to the children and to the forest. They ring with her "feeling so deeply that [she is] startled into a different level of awareness." They ring with the ways in which Shelley shows up with as much awareness and willing vulnerability as she can muster.

In Shelley's presence, her awareness, her vulnerability, we see the crack appear – the crack of Shelley's heart breaking open. And what light shines through that crack! The light of tenderness and empathy, humility and self-awareness, courage and tears and surprising new perspectives.

---

1) Leonard Cohen, "Anthem" on the album *The Future*, 1992

Shelley's heart breaks open when a child she'd taught dies and her family tells Shelley that her documentation stories about their child's short, exuberant life are a source of comfort in their crushing grief.

Shelley's heart breaks open when she watches a two-year-old embrace a dying tree, and, with her caress and her whispered words of comfort, honor the wrecked tree and honor what it means to care for a tree.

Shelley's heart breaks open when she and her group of toddlers inadvertently crush snails hidden in the grass underfoot as they walk the familiar path to the forest. And her heart breaks open some more when the children lean close to the living snails that they *do* see, chatting cheerfully with them as they watch them creep across the path and up the stalks of flowers.

Each time Shelley's heart cracks open, light gets in, illuminating an expanded understanding of what it means to be a teacher. "The educator part of me had forgotten the human part of me, the part that draws me in close to experiences and holds me there," Shelley writes.

> Heartbreak reconnects me to the human experience and invites me to look beyond the analytical side of learning. Heartbreak invites me to quiet my mind and to consider a child's heart. As an educator, reimagining heartbreak affords me the courage and

foreword

curiosity to look beyond formal assessments and see children for the whole-hearted humans that they are.

This is not how we typically talk about our work as educators. We too often border our hearts, thinking we ought to hold ourselves at some distance from the children, from the life we share with the children – or, when that proves impossible, believing we ought at least to refrain from talking about our hearts. How have we allowed that border to take such firm hold in our field? Perhaps we've convinced ourselves that it's more "professional" to keep our focus squarely on children's learning, to keep ourselves out of the picture.

Shelley reminds us that we don't have to choose between being either *an educator* or *a human*. That looks preposterous when it's said plainly, doesn't it? It's not a dichotomy, but, rather, an integration of identity and role. Being an educator is a way to express – and to nourish – our human being-ness. As educators, we bring our human selves to our days with children, keeping company with children's human selves. When we let our hearts break open, the light that gets in illuminates our shared humanity.

"Because children grow up, we think a child's purpose is to grow up," Tom Stoppard wrote[2]. "But a child's purpose is to be a child." Shelley's stories remind us that we align

---

2) Tom Stoppard, *The Coast of Utopia*, Grove Press, 2007.

ourselves with a child's purpose when we tune ourselves to their whole-hearted living. We spend our days with babies and young children, people who have been alive on this planet for only a few years, new to this world and deserving of our open hearts. They deserve to be seen as "the whole-hearted humans that they are." We sorely disrespect children when we constrict our gaze to their academic learning or developmental accomplishments.

And with this limited gaze, we disrespect ourselves, too. Alongside her embrace of children's whole-heartedness, Shelley makes a promise to herself to reclaim her whole-heartedness, an act of deep regard for her right to show up as her full human self as an educator. Witnessing the children's whole-heartedness, Shelley longs for "the bravery to be true to myself, the humility of knowing that I am part of something bigger. I am motivated to be a more complete version of myself, a version that is fully engaged and present, a version that feels fully and cares relentlessly." And she answers that longing by saying *Yes. I will grow into that person, and be that person with children.*

To become that person, Shelley studies herself and her responses to the children, a commitment at the heart of what our profession calls "reflective practice."

We often toss off the line that "Children have so much to teach us." Shelley offers us a potent way to understand the learning that is available to us adults.

foreword

As an educator, I sometimes forget that I am not the only one watching. While my attention is focused on the little ones, their attention is just as focused on me. And as they watch me, they pick up on things: subtleties of my character, my mannerisms, my habits, the things that make me smile.

Then, in those moments when my attention is ripe, they offer something back to me about myself, something I might not have noticed otherwise. I see hints of how they define me; how they understand who I am; how they identify me as part of their world. Almost always it catches me off guard. It startles me to bear witness to a child's understanding of my character, a child's translation of my words.

When we attune ourselves to the children with our hearts open, we discover aspects of our character, our human selves, that we may not have seen before. We see what the children see in us: what they perceive that we value, what they perceive delights us, what they perceive unsettles us. And this is where our learning lies: we can "think more deeply about how these moments that [we] share with children influence [us as educators, as humans.]"

And we also can learn from children about expansive, whole-hearted living, reclaiming that capacity for ourselves: "the feeling of being in complete and utter awe of something, the innocence of watching something new and unfamiliar unfold, the pure joy found in uninterrupted experience. ... What it is like to feel deep connections to the natural world."

Teacher and pedagogical coach Susan Harris MacKay writes[3]

> Most of us long for things we've lost since we were children: our sense of wonder, our powerful imagination, our willing curiosity. When we listen to children, we remember the promise those gifts hold – for the individual and for the community and for the world. When we listen to our own curiosity, wonder, and imagination, when we rekindle those gifts for ourselves, we make it possible for the children we care for to sustain theirs – and we make the world we want to live in together.

We make the world we want to live in together – a world in which we comfort broken trees, chat with snails, listen for the owl in the forest. We make the world we want to live in together – a world in which we share joyful stories as gestures of comfort in times of grief. We make the world we want to live in together –

---

[3] Susan Harris MacKay, The Center for Playful Inquiry website
www.centerforplayfulinquiry.com

foreword

a world in which we listen to each other with empathy and humility and kindness.

The stories in this book come from a transformational shift in how Shelley understands pedagogical documentation. Her former documentation practice focused solely on the children. Now, she includes herself in the stories, "describing how a child's actions affected me, how a simple encounter mattered to my heart." This isn't the typical way that educators write for families. Shelley recognizes there is no such thing as being "objective" in our writing or in our teaching; she acknowledges that "I have an undeniable role in the stories that emerge from my days with children." Documentation that truly matters for the children, their families, and for educators reveals self-awareness, open-heartedness, new insights and wonderings. Shelley positions herself to write from her heart because it "affords me the courage and guided curiosity to look beyond formal assessments and see children for the whole-hearted humans that they are. ... When I connect to my own heart, I become more aware of the children's hearts."

What a gift to offer families – the gift of whole-hearted presence to and witness of their children! And what a necessary challenge to the idea that families want our documentation stories to be reports on their children's learning, or on how the children are meeting developmental markers. Shelley reminds us that, when our stories "capture their children's spirits in a genuine way," our stories can be "a source of comfort" to parents. And when we allow ourselves to be seen in what we write, our stories can be steadying and grounding for families, opportunities for them to know us better – to learn how we think about children, what we care about, what breaks our hearts open. This is surely a source of comfort as they entrust their children into our care.

Comfort from whole-heartedness, from hearts broken open. Light shining through the cracks. Heartbreak is surely an experience for each of us, for all of us, in this life. The heartbreak of a sorely damaged planet. The heartbreak of fascism's resurgence. The heartbreak of persistent injustice and oppression, of racist violence, and the violence of poverty and inequity. The heartbreak of knowing that each of these forces will impact the unfolding lives of children. Open hearts are what will carry us onward – open hearts that allow us to feel fully and tenderly and courageously. Open hearts that hold space for hope as a moral commitment to stay present in the face of heartbreak.

Buddhist teacher Pema Chödrön writes[4] that, "When we don't close off and we let our hearts break, we discover our kinship with all beings. ... Whenever we look at the world around us, whenever we connect with sorrow, whenever we connect with joy ... in those moments, *bodhichitta* (tenderness for life) is here."

---

4) Pema Chödrön *When Things Fall Apart*, Shambhala Press, 2016.

foreword

Tenderness for life. Kinship with all beings. This is the light that will illuminate our way forward. Shelley's stories bring alive the experience of kinship: toddlers, the trees and other beings who inhabit the forest, and Shelley, made kin by whole-heartedness. There is no more perfect offering than presence, no more perfect offering than opening ourselves to sorrow and joy, no more perfect offering than our hearts.

> *Ring the bells that still can ring*
> *Forget your perfect offering*
> *There is a crack, a crack in everything*
> *That's how the light gets in.*

—Ann Pelo and Margie Carter
Editors of the *Reimagining Our Work* (ROW) Collection

Authors of *From Teaching to Thinking: A Pedagogy for Reimagining Our Work*

introduction

I first meet Aleena when she joins my group as a young toddler. She is tall for her age and her lanky frame plays tricks on her balance. But she has a glint in her eye that confirms an undeniable determination to live fully into every experience.

One of the first things Aleena notices in our outdoor space is our collection of stumps and logs. They vary in size and stability, which provides both challenge and possibility for toddlers. Right away, Aleena races over to the stumps and starts to explore. I watch her drape her limbs and contort her body in the most peculiar ways as she struggles to get up on a stump. I am nervous watching her maneuver her body, and, because I'm just getting to know her, I am certainly more fearful for her than she is! I want to protect her, but at the same time, I want to give her the chance to climb on her own. So, with trepidation, I step back and cautiously look on. She grips the edge of the stump and braces her torso against it. As she leans forward, her weight shifts and she loses her grip. She stumbles and I lunge forward with my arms outstretched to stop her fall.

As anxious as I feel, she is unfazed by her spill and seems willing to accept that setbacks like this are a necessary part of progress. She scrambles to her feet and repositions herself against the stump. Slowly, methodically, she renews her ascent, clutching the stump tighter when it wobbles, and steadying her body against it. She finally gets her legs up and squats low to maintain her balance. At this point, she pauses, as if to give herself a moment to acclimatize to her new position. Bit by bit, she begins to unfold her body. Her legs, shaky at first, straighten and stabilize. With arms stretched out to her sides, she hovers, bent over at the waist. Slowly, she stands upright, and raises her hands above her head in celebration of her achievement. However, the triumph is cut short when the stump starts to wobble again. She quickly shifts her weight and manages to maintain her precarious perch. Already demonstrating more confidence than just seconds before, she shoots upwards once again.

As it turns out, Aleena is a powerhouse climber! Her nimble body seems to be designed for climbing, and this, combined with her fearless determination, makes for abundant success. I am glad that I resisted the urge to 'save' her during her first climbing attempt; by holding back, I was able to witness how capable she is when it comes to climbing. Seeing how methodical and cautious she is in her approach settles my nerves, and I feel like I can finally breathe again.

Aleena, the Mud Splasher

Our centre has declared one day early in the summer to be a celebration of the power of puddles and the marvels of mud. We've transformed the play yard into a landscape of water and mud, and invited the children to Mud Day!

Aleena is quick to position herself in the middle of the action, as children splash and spray mud all around her. As soon as her feet hit the water, she starts to giggle – it is surprising that such a thunderous eruption could burst out of this slight little being! She is dripping wet and her mud-caked ringlets playfully bounce and stretch down her back. When she runs through the sprinklers, her giggle becomes even more pronounced, and everyone around her starts to laugh, too. Aleena brings a playful, joyful energy to our group, and as I witness her in this moment, I cannot help but be joyful, too.

I watch her run towards a deep mud puddle that has formed from a slow leak in the garden hose. The water is icy cold, so there are more onlookers than puddle-jumpers. This won't last long, though, because here comes Aleena, aiming to make an enormous SPLASH! As her feet land in the puddle at its deepest point, murky water blasts upwards like a geyser. I lose sight of Aleena for a moment as the puddle morphs into a tsunami that completely engulfs her slender frame. The wave subsides and she emerges, saturated. She stands in the chilly water, soaked and shivering, as water trickles down her body and leaves muddy trails from her head down to her toes. I think about rushing in to wrap her in a towel and shelter her from the dampness and chill, but instead, I wait. I am curious to see how she responds and I want to give her the space to appreciate the whole puddle experience without my interference. And I am not disappointed. Aleena's eyes widen and she starts to giggle again, and that quickly turns into a full-blown belly laugh. Suddenly, the hesitant puddle onlookers join in on the fun. I'm glad I resisted the impulse to swoop in and hurry her out of the cold water; when I held myself back, I got to know Aleena better.

introduction

Aleena, the Observer

On a visit to the forest, Aleena strolls along at a slow pace well behind the other children. She takes her time to caress the flowers, to admire the bees, to gaze up at the geese flying overhead. I find myself watching her every move, compelled by the way that she relates so intimately with the creatures and the plants she encounters, the way she can be so still for so long. When a slow-moving snail catches her eye, she flops to the ground for a closer look, stretching out on the path to study the snail.

I study Aleena.

When she notices the shimmering slime trail that the snail leaves in its wake, she looks up at me with wide eyes, amazement in her gaze. I can see that she has questions, that she wonders about this sparkling line drawn by the snail, but I don't say anything. I feel as though any response from me could disrupt this beautiful encounter between Aleena and the snail, so I decide to stay silent. There will be plenty of time to hypothesize and research when we return to the centre this afternoon, I think to myself.

Aleena stays with the snail for a long time, and parts ways with it only after it has safely made it to the other side of the path. She scrambles to her feet , then crouches down to whisper a final message before skipping off to meet up with the group: "Good-bye, snail! Have a nice trip!"

Aleena, Lover of Life

There is something about Aleena.

She has an energy that pulls me in, and she inspires me to move through the world with my eyes wide and my heart poised to crack open at any second. She is strong and resilient, gentle and sincere. She is a lover of all things. The tiniest beetle, the most colourful butterfly, the muddiest puddle, the broken and discarded dandelion: everything seems to hold a special place in her heart. She radiates kindness and compassion towards everything and everyone she encounters. She wears her heart on her sleeve.

In many ways, she reminds me of the way I used to be as a child.

After three years together, it was time for Aleena to leave our centre for kindergarten. I remember Aleena's preschool farewell like it was yesterday. At our goodbye ritual at the classroom door, nostalgia inspired waterworks for both of us. I recalled the awkwardly tall, beautifully courageous child who had entered my toddler group a few years prior, and I was consumed with a fiery pride, an acknowledgement that I held a significant place in her story. As we flipped through the archived stories in her portfolio, we shared memories of our adventures together. I hoped that the stories I had written echoed her true character and that the photos captured her unwavering sense of adventure. A tearful hug cemented our farewell and I watched Aleena skip through our doors one last time.

An Unexpected Farewell
Nothing could have prepared me for the news of Aleena's sudden illness and death a few months later. It didn't make any sense to me: this spirited, joyful, lover of life, abruptly gone from the world. I was numb, in disbelief. My heart ached for her family.

I hadn't seen Aleena since that end-of-summer farewell ritual at our classroom door, so I didn't expect her family to contact me, but they did.

And I will never forget that phone call.

Aleena's mom asked me to speak at Aleena's memorial service, to celebrate the vibrancy and sparkle that Aleena brought to life. And so I did. I talked about her ever-present smile, that cheerful giggle, and her love for every adventure that presented itself. I shared stories of our time together, stories of forest walks, tales of tender moments. Her stories. My stories. Our stories.

Her mom told me that she turned to Aleena's portfolio as a source of comfort in her grief. She thanked me for writing stories about her little girl, about our adventures, because those stories captured her daughter's spirit in a genuine way. Realizing how crucial these stories were for

Aleena's family suddenly made them more valuable to me, too. I started to think more deeply about how these moments that I share with children influence me as an educator, as a human.

Aleena inspires me to reclaim whole-heartedness

After Aleena died, I changed the way I approached documenting stories about the children. I started to include myself in my writing: describing how a child's actions affected me, how a simple encounter mattered to my heart. I used Aleena's stories as a reference point because I saw Aleena so vividly within that writing, and I started to see myself more clearly, too.

Before meeting Aleena, I don't recall that I paid much attention to my side of the educator-child relationship. I gave very little thought to how I was – or could be – influenced by the actions of a young child. But there was something about Aleena that made me want to watch more closely, something that made me want to get down on the ground and quietly witness the splendor of a toddler engaging with the natural world.

Aleena reminded me of me.

What I saw in Aleena conjured up memories from my own childhood: the feeling of being in complete and utter awe of something, the innocence of watching something new and unfamiliar unfold, the pure joy found in uninterrupted experience. Watching Aleena, admiring her, reminded me what it was like to move through life guided by my heart, to feel deep connections to the natural world, just as I did when I was a child.

The exuberant anticipation of a monumental mud splash, the quiet comfort of keeping solitary company with a snail, the power of feeling strong and confident scaling a stump – these moments with Aleena awakened something within me. This, I concluded, was what had been missing for me: a commitment to embrace the emotional swells of my heart. The educator part of me had forgotten the human part of me, the part that draws me in close to experiences and holds me there. My life with Aleena, and her death, inspired within me a promise to reclaim whole-heartedness in my life as an educator.

And here's where that promise carries me:

- Being with children whole-heartedly makes me long for things: the feeling of being young again, the bravery to be true to myself, the humility of knowing that I am part of something bigger. I am motivated to be a more complete version of myself, a version that is fully engaged and present, a version that feels fully and cares relentlessly. And when I am with the little ones, our experiences together awaken me to a flood of emotions so raw and pure that I am almost always left wanting more.

- Being with children whole-heartedly engages my emotions. They linger closer to the surface and my emotions are more centered in my thoughts, my experiences, my responses to the children. I embrace the jolts and the jars, the swells and the constrictions that come with feeling deeply and fully. Giving attention to my emotions has begun to shape me into the kind of educator I have always longed to be: a passion-driven, eyes-wide-open, heart-on-my-sleeve, aware, alert, responsive educator, ready to take on the world alongside a group of little ones with their fresh perspectives and insights.

- Being with children prompts me to study myself and my responses. What exactly is it that I am experiencing? What happens when I start to feel so deeply about something that I am startled into a different level of awareness? What is it that I am feeling?

Stories Centred in Heartbreak

For me, whole-heartedness – the feeling of my heart bursting open – serves as a portal to experiencing life and living, with robust attention and commitment to being present. This alertness makes me more receptive, more responsive to the spirit of the moment that plays out in front of me. As an educator – as a human – it serves as a reminder for me to feel, to express, to reflect on those beautiful moments shared with children, moments that reconnect me to a place of heightened awareness, to a time when my heart centred me in my experiences.

The stories in this collection are about heartbreak, but not heartbreak in the typical sense. Instead, I reimagine heartbreak as a breaking-open of my heart, into new possibilities. *What if I break open my heart in order to learn something about myself, to elicit an emotional response that I hadn't experienced before? What if I break open my heart to expose my vulnerabilities, to stir my emotions and make me a more engaged, attentive educator, and human? What if I break open my heart to create time and space to linger in the swell of emotions?*

I think about Aleena often when I write stories for children's portfolios. I think about the stories that I wrote about her, and how they came to mean so much to her family. I think about her when my heart bursts wide open and my sensitivities become my guide, because she reminded me to embrace those deep feelings. My stories come from a different place now.

I write from my heart.

I declare my place in the story because, as an educator, I am part of the shared experience. I have decided to tell stories about the beautiful moments that break open my heart. When I connect to my own heart in this way, I become more aware of the children's hearts.

reimagining heartbreak

Heartbreak reconnects me to the human experience and invites me to look beyond the analytical side of learning. Heartbreak invites me to quiet my mind and to consider a child's heart. As an educator, reimagining heartbreak affords me the courage and guided curiosity to look beyond formal assessments and see children for the whole-hearted humans that they are.

Heartbreak doesn't mean the end of something.

In fact, for me heartbreak is just the beginning.

introduction

CHAPTER 1

the forest as home ground

The forest is my happy place; it always has been. I go there to recalibrate myself, to experience the liveliness, to embrace the solitude. Like a metronome, the forest sets my rhythm, so I proceed steady and sure, confident and courageous. I go there to reminisce: some of my fondest childhood memories are of times spent in the forest foraging for morels, harvesting wild leeks, going on long walks with my family. I carry these memories with me: memories of an uncomplicated, unhurried presence and a deep kinship with the land. The forest nourishes my soul. It is my faithful companion, my ubiquitous ally. My heart lives in the forest.

Twenty-five years ago, I stumbled into a career in early childhood education, and over the years I have made it my priority to engage with children in outdoor experiences and adventures. The city where I live is a rapidly expanding urban centre, so it has not always been easy to find naturally-occurring forest spaces where little ones were welcome to explore. But as luck would have it, a few years back I had the opportunity to relocate to a new childcare centre, a site that was attached to a brand-new elementary school. It was built in the first phase of the development of a new suburban neighbourhood, and in those early days we were surrounded by farms, fields and forests. It was like a dream! However, over time, the farms and fields were swallowed up by single family dwellings: row upon row of nearly identical homes, built within inches of each other. I worried about the future of our forest spaces, especially the one that we visited most often that sat adjacent to our school. What would come of it? Would it find permanence in the midst of this concrete chaos? Thankfully, this particular tract of land was gifted to the city, which prevented housing developers from infringing on its boundaries. The community grew up around it, and for us, the forest has become a central place for outdoor exploration with our toddlers.

Our group – myself, another forest-loving educator, and five adventure-seeking toddlers at a time – visits the forest regularly, regardless of weather. The space provides us with a place to wander and wonder. It is not an expansive lot, certainly not isolated or rugged, but it is a lively little place and it is just the right size for us.

Over time, we have discovered cherished spots among the trees:

spots where we can linger, spots we want to keep secret, spots that we hold dear to our hearts. We have grown to love a handful of trees in particular, and these trees possess unique qualities or conjure up specific memories for us: there is the "owl tree," and the "sideways tree," and the "hot chocolate tree." These places are familiar to all of us and when we are there, we fall effortlessly into our explorations.

The Hot Chocolate Tree

On one of our forest walks, the group decides to stop at the "hot chocolate tree." Right away we begin to toss around memories of that snowy day a few weeks back when this tree acquired its unique name.

There is a chill in the air, and that, paired with the overnight snowfall, creates an idyllic backdrop for today's visit to the forest. We had made hot chocolate to take with us, the perfect wintery treat. As we begin the trek across the field to the forest, the tacky snow fuses to our boots and slows us to a frustrating crawl. The forest is not that far away, but just steps into our trip, we are covered with snow and already feeling its frosty grasp. The only thing that keeps us moving forward is the promise of the cocoa.

My initial plan was to lead the group deep into the forest, perhaps to a clearing under last year's owl nest. In my mind, that would be the perfect place to roll out a blanket and enjoy our sweet snack. However, the journey across the field proves to be much more difficult than I'd anticipated, and the resulting snow-filled boots and soggy mittens require us to modify our plan. I invite the group to choose a spot somewhere closer to the edge of the forest where we can sit for a moment. With a surge of renewed energy, the group runs ahead, fueled by their assignment to find the best spot. Moments later, the forest fills with excited shrieks and beckoning waves, as the children urge me to hurry and join them: they have decided on a 'hot chocolate tree.'

I spread the blanket on the snow and the children start to pile on. One by one, the toddlers claim their spot in a semicircle around the edge and stretch their legs towards the centre of the blanket. I drop my backpack in the snow and start to unpack it. Cheers erupt at the sight of the thermos! I twist off its lid and wafts of chocolate-scented steam escape into the air. The smell is accentuated when I pour our decadent brew into the child-sized mugs that we've lined up in the snow. We have to wait until it cools, I explain, and I suggest that they could go explore the forest while we wait. But everyone stays still on the blanket, their eyes fixed on the steaming mugs nestled in the snow. Finally, after what seems like forever, we distribute the mugs and for the next few minutes slurps and chugs, smacking lips and satisfying sighs become our language. I sense that this will be the first of many visits to this tree; today's experience has the making of a beautiful memory for us all!

Back in the forest, we share stories of that snowy day, as we linger under our 'hot chocolate tree.' This will be our jumping-off point for our explorations today; the children know precisely where they want to channel their attention. In an instant they scatter, and I am left on my own, challenged to discover my own direction. The group is thoroughly engaged, so much so that I think they may have forgotten that I am even here! It's a welcome break from the typical intensity and energy, and I feel that I can let my guard down a bit to pause and savour the moment. The lull of toddler chatter and giggles is almost meditative, and, as I watch the children from a respectful distance, I allow my mind to wander. Soon, I am satisfied to be lost in my own thoughts and queries. I settle into my own rhythm and start to explore.

reimagining heartbreak

> *I am surprised by an emotional swell that rises in my heart.*

I think about how the children gathered around the 'hot chocolate tree' for the first time, and am overcome with nostalgia. I see myself as a young child, trudging through the forest on a crisp and cool winter's day. I feel a profound sense of longing: my childhood has roots in the forest, and I begin to connect my own early experiences with the joyful encounters that are unfolding in front of me.

I am about eight or nine years old. My mom and I stand at the kitchen window and stare out at the freshly fallen snow. It snowed a lot overnight, enough to cover all the deep plough ruts in the field behind our house. It is sunny and bright, and the snow glistens. We decide that it is a perfect day to go cross country skiing. My dad is clearing some logs in the forest at the back of our property, so our plan is to surprise him where he's working. We quickly piece together a modest lunch and brew up a thermos of hot cocoa. We dress in our warmest sweaters, and layer Dad's old wool work socks over ours, then pull on our outer waterproof layers. Our ski boots have definitely seen better days, but the extra sock layers will keep our toes toasty on our trip.

Finally, clipped into our skis, with our packs strapped on our backs, we head towards the forest.

The trip today is challenging: the snow creates the illusion that the fields are flat, but the landscape that is hidden underneath is deeply rutted, with ragged furrows from the plough. We falter, we flop into the snow, we struggle to reclaim our footing. The trip seems to take forever, and we are both beginning to feel the chill of the snow seeping into our boots. But we finally reach the edge of the forest, and from there, the buzz of Dad's chainsaw guides us into the trees.

Densely packed evergreens skirt the edges of the path. Fragrant cedar boughs stretch out over the trail and swat my cold-blushed cheeks as I pass by. The steep hills, sudden turns, and buried tree roots knock me off my feet more than once. As we move further into the forest, the sound of the chainsaw gets louder and now the air reeks of sawdust and fuel oil. There's another smell, though: something familiar, yet out of place. I glide around the final corner of the trail and there it is: the most spectacular bonfire I have ever seen, flames licking and sparks jumping, IN THE SNOW! This fiery bliss, nestled among the trees, astonishes me. Who knew that you could build a campfire in the snow? It takes my breath away.

My mom and I lean our skis up against a tree and sit down on stumps close to the fire. Flames warm my toes. The snow around the fire sizzles and steams, and as it melts, it exposes the ground. Heat sears my frost-kissed cheeks and the billowing smoke stings my watering eyes. And I am happy. We open our picnic lunch, which happens to be hot dogs that we roast over the bonfire! We sip our hot cocoa and the aroma of rich, dark chocolate marries beautifully with the sweet smokiness of the fire. It is absolutely magical.

As I stand in our little forest watching the toddlers explore and remembering that winter campfire so many years ago, I swear that I can smell the crackling wood. For a second, I am that younger version of myself tucked in next to that bonfire in the snow, creating my own "hot chocolate tree" story.

My memories reunite me with the emotions from that snowheld campfire with my parents.

I wonder what stories these children will remember years from now.

What kinds of tales will they tell about our forest adventures together and time spent underneath our precious "hot chocolate tree?" I hope they recall the challenging journey through the sticky snow, and the joy when they declared their "hot chocolate tree" because this will reconnect them to a beloved place. I hope they remember the scent of chocolate billowing from the thermos, and the way the snow melted under our steaming mugs so they are reminded of that feeling of anticipation when their lives seem predictable and mundane. I hope they hear the laughter and the excited shrieks from their friends, a joyful reminder of the value of relationships.

And I hope they see me there, too.

CHAPTER 2

the teacher

We enter the forest just as we do every other day. I take the lead initially, as always, pausing at the section of downed fencing to step slowly across into the forest. As the children follow me across the fence, I am aware of the shift in energy, and in leadership. The children recognize this threshold. In the short time we have been visiting the forest, they have come to know this place well.

I feel their confidence.

I sense their anticipation.

I notice the silent yet palpable shift in their awareness and attention.

I feel the shift in myself, too.

I pause for a moment to breathe in the damp mustiness of the forest and scan the terrain. The forest is alive and it has its own stories to share. I can feel it in the air: today is going to be a good day.

With each step we take, the delicate ice underfoot declares its fragility, crackling and crumbling as it succumbs to the heavy burden our boots place upon it. Twisted knots of withered undergrowth mask the maze under the snow and snare us often and unexpectedly as we pass. Beams of sunlight stretch down through the gnarled limbs and entangled monkey vines above us, warming the crisp morning air to a tolerable temperature. The forest landscape is muted, brownish grey, and the spatters of ice and snow remind us that spring is yet to come.

I pause to whisper a quiet greeting to our special place.

A surge of energy whizzes by me and jolts me back into the moment. It is one of the children, bursting with confidence and curiosity, and eager to begin today's adventure. He flashes a quick grin as he passes, as if to say, "I've got this." He marches onward, ahead of me. A few yards past me, he stops and turns abruptly, facing me with his arm outstretched in the universal signal for "Stop."

"Wait," he demands. "I'm gonna be the teacher today."

I wonder what this might look like and how I ought to respond; then it occurs to me that he is not asking my permission to lead. This is his declaration. The *Teacher* has a plan.

And he has my full attention.

He turns and starts to carve a path in the fresh snow. He has his sights set on a sturdy old tree a few paces in and heads towards it. Curious, I follow along, as do the others.

"Come over here," he says. "Feel this tree."

He bites at the tips of his mittens and they drop to his feet. Barehanded now, he reaches out and caresses the tree. Without a second thought, I follow his lead and reach out towards the tree. The bark is rough, almost jagged to the touch, and it snags my wool mittens.

"There's lots of bumps here... big ones and little ones, too. Isn't that cool?"

He looks at me and nods his head, encouraging me to respond.

> *This is my invitation to explore more deeply,*

so I drop my mittens to the ground and touch the tree. I don't speak. I notice the details of the bark more than ever. I have touched the bark of trees before, and traced the tightly spun loops and whorls of knots with my fingertips. But his summons to attend to details of the trees intrigues me. The way he coaxes me to notice the lumps and bumps sets this experience apart from my other encounters with bark. This feels different. But why?

I begin to settle into this question, curious to understand the distinction between this experience and ones I have had in the past. Part of me wants to stop, right here, right now, to make some sense of what's going on for me. But what might I miss? What might I discover? There's no time to linger. The *Teacher* moves on, and I follow.

We arrive at another tree. "This one has stripes," he says. "I wonder how that happened." I wonder about that, too, I think to myself. The *Teacher* looks at me, his eyes set on mine. He does not seek approval; likewise, he does not seek a definitive response. The *Teacher* invites me into his world, in the same way I have so often invited him into mine. We continue to study the bark patterns together, silently. I feel a powerful connection to the moment, to him. I hear myself in him; the words he chooses, the way he says things. His words are my words. His tone echoes familiarity.

We continue our journey through the snow, weaving a path from one tree to the next. The *Teacher* leads, and the rest of us happily follow. The next tree that we encounter has some unique features, too. The *Teacher* stops in front of it and stares closely at its bark. He reaches out and caresses the tree with his fingertips.

"This one has cuts in it...like from a knife or something." The *Teacher* looks at me with that same inviting glance as before. Grinning, he shrugs his shoulders a few times. I feel a wave of emotion come over me and I smile.

He gets his shoulder shrug from me.

The *Teacher* has been watching me, listening to me, during our weeks together.

He has been studying the way I speak, the way I respond, the way I am, with him and with others.

I see it so clearly here in the forest. It is beautiful and touching and it stirs my heart.

The *Teacher* calls to me; he has moved on to the next tree with the group, and I hurry to catch up.

"This one's pretty cool, too. It has lots of holes in it. Maybe a mouse did it...or a rabbit...maybe even a crocodile."

I offer him an approving nod and a slight smile, and...

Wait...what did he say? A crocodile?

I look to him with surprise, and I am met with a playful grin and that trademark shoulder shrug. He was just making sure I was still listening! He must have sensed that my attention was slipping.

We continue through the forest, stopping often to explore the textures of trees. The *Teacher* is our guide and he takes his role very seriously. I do, too, and I attend to his monologue with a humble intensity. I have become aware that his words and actions offer a reflection of myself back to me for study. I listen with an open heart, and acknowledge the rhythms of my own words in how he speaks. I watch with a fiery presence because I know that he sometimes moves like I do and it brings me such joy that I do not want to miss it when it happens again. I see a bit of myself in him and it makes me glow.

As an educator, I sometimes forget that I am not the only one watching. While my attention is focused on the little ones, their attention is just as focused on me.

And as they watch me, they pick up on things: subtleties of my character, my mannerisms, my habits, the things that make me smile.

Then, in those moments when my attention is ripe, they offer something back to me about myself, something I might not have noticed otherwise. I see hints of how they define me; how they understand who I am; how they identify me as part of their world. Almost always it catches me off guard. It startles me to bear witness to a child's understanding of my character, a child's translation of my words.

Today's glimpse of myself helps me realize that

I have an undeniable role in the stories that emerge from my days with children, whether I am leading or following.

Through the actions and words of my two-year-old *Teacher – a Teacher* whose life experiences total less than one thousand days – I saw a version of myself that made me proud. I saw an image of how I want others to see me; as someone who inspires and is inspired by others to lean in and offer attention to tree bark and bramble; as someone who ponders rather than poses questions, someone who invites rather than interrogates.

CHAPTER 3

the gift

There is a definite chill in the air this morning as we begin our daily pilgrimage to the forest. The leafless trees make it seem much colder than it actually is, and that, mixed with the dull skies and distant rumbles, have me wondering what, if anything, we will get from today's journey.

Leaves are scattered across the forest floor like a tattered old tapestry in shades of red, brown, orange and yellow.

They blanket the ground and cover the lumps, bumps and divots that I might ordinarily see. As we walk, sticks and twigs crunch under my feet. It is hard to see them; the leaves camouflage all but the occasional branch. My foot gets snagged when I least expect it, and prompts me to remember the landscape that hides from sight.

I notice a gnarled and weathered stick poking out from under the leaves. I pick it up, brush away the clumps of damp soil, and break off a few small twigs. The stick is much taller than me and really bowed in the middle. It bends and gives with even the slightest bit of pressure. I decide to hang onto it, at least for now, to walk with it for a while.

After a few minutes, though, I realize how awkward this stick feels in my hand. It bends almost to the point of breaking. It twists in my grip and pinches the tender flesh of my palm. And its surface is so rough! It is scratchy and damp and warped, and not at all pleasant to hold. This stick does not make a satisfying companion at all. I drop it at my side and continue walking.

Not too long afterwards, another stick presents itself to me. It's a little straighter than the last one, and definitely stronger. It has a pronounced bow in its middle, too, but it seems to hold up well when I push down on it. I brush off the damp soil and musty leaves, and start to walk, poking the end of the stick into the soil with each step. It's definitely not perfect, but it will do for now.

the gift

By now I am trailing behind the rest of the group as they zig and zag among the trees. When I finally catch up to them, I jab the pointed end of my stick into the ground. This catches one of the children's attention, and she turns and walks over to me. She looks the stick up and down, then locks eyes with me.

She gestures at the stick and asks, "What's that for?"

"It's my walking stick," I explain. "I use it to help keep my balance." My words spark a sharp silence, as the children begin to scrutinize the forest floor. They scan the ground for any stick that they could use. Boots disrupt the layers of leaves, releasing the pungent fragrance of leaf rot. The children scoop up sticks, and poke with them at the ground to test the strength and durability of their selections. They drop sticks and choose new ones. They poke at the ground again, rating their new choice against some secret list of walking stick criteria that only they know. Sticks are discovered, displaced, tested, and discarded. Eventually, each child finds their own version of the perfect walking stick. I am thrilled that they show such an interest in choosing their own walking sticks.

It is an opportunity for them to see the individual characteristics that each stick possesses.

and it shifts their attention away from seeing sticks only as objects that poke us and trip us and litter our path.

We return to our walk through the forest, armed with our new wooden companions. But I am not settled with my stick. It is not quite as long as I want it to be and I have to hunch over to use it, and that impairs my ability to fully enjoy our walk. I appreciate my chosen stick less and less with every passing second. Soon enough, I toss it aside – and in that very moment, I notice a new one, a better one, right at my feet! Pleased with my new selection, I continue to walk, but before long, I start to find faults in this stick, too. The curve is too pronounced and the stick is jabbing into my hand. I try to make it work, but this stick is causing physical pain. It has to go.

I start to lag behind the group again as I struggle to find the perfect stick to accompany me on our journey. The toddlers notice this and they pause, waiting for me to catch up. I quickly select another stick, for no reason other than that it happens to be at my feet. This one will have to do.

I know that I am being very particular about my choice, and I am not sure why. I am also aware that the children are watching, and I don't want my indecision to start a 'thing' where the children are stalled in their search for 'perfect.' I recognize that they are taking time to notice the subtleties of each stick, but I do not want them to become so preoccupied with this task that they forget to enjoy their time in the forest.

I walk on, carrying my latest stick, but I'm distracted. The stick is too light, too long, too sharp at the end. I try my best not to let this awkward, pointy, lanky twig of a stick get the better of me,

not wanting the children to see me still fussing about my stick.

Inevitably, though, the stick wins, and I discreetly drop it on the forest floor when no one is looking.

I try to convince myself that I am done with sticks for the day, but every now and then I catch myself scanning the ground again. The children must see it, too; when they call to me, they must see that my eyes are trained on the forest floor rather than taking in whatever they are trying to show me. I am missing out on their moments and I am well aware of that, but despite myself, I am having a hard time abandoning my search for the perfect stick. I feel discontented and disconnected.

It's unsettling.

This certainly is not the way I wanted our walk to be today.

Then I feel someone standing close to me. I turn, and there she is, a couple of steps behind me. She is clutching a stick in her hands, and as she comes closer, she holds it up towards me.

"Look at this!" she says, offering her stick to me for inspection.

"Oh, that is a nice stick! It's long, and bumpy and has lots of curves!" I reply. I assume that concludes our exchange, that she is going to race past me to join her friends. Instead, she holds her place beside me. And what she says next melts my heart.

"I found it for you," she says, and she places the stick in my open hands. Without further explanation, she flashes a cheerful smile and races by me to join the group.

I am left speechless, standing frozen in place, cradling this most beautiful walking stick in my hands. It is long, but not too long; weighty without being burdensome. The curve on the top nestles into my palm at precisely the right spot and the grip itself is smooth and free of knots. The stick is gnarled and warped, a stretch of curves, twists and straightaways that runs all the way to the pointed tip at the ground. It is a swirled palette of taupe and brown, spotted with random ebony whirls. The outer layer of bark has been sloughed away, and the stick that is left behind has a glossy, weathered sheen, almost as if it had been coated in lacquer. It is beautiful in every way. This stick feels perfect in my hands!

She had been watching me struggle to find the stick that checked all the right boxes. She had no way to tell what criteria I was using to make my choices. But she had been noticing me in my unsatisfying quest for a stick – and that mattered to me.

Perhaps she noticed that my attention was drifting away from the group. Or maybe she noticed that I was frustrated. Whatever it was that caught her attention, it had inspired her to abandon her search for a stick for herself to prioritize finding a stick for me.

I look at this stick – this perfect walking stick – and my heart breaks.

I feel such gratitude that this child noticed my struggles and offered me a gift that pulled me back into the moment.

This stick was just an ordinary stick a few moments ago, one of thousands scattered across the forest floor. But now this stick is extraordinary! This stick is perfect because it was chosen especially for me, gifted to me out of thoughtfulness and care, by a child who, at barely three years old, already knows me so well.

As an educator, I see myself as a companion to children. I accompany them through our daily experiences and support them as they learn and grow. But they are companions to my own experiences and learning, too.

I don't always acknowledge how much I am influenced by the actions and responses of these little ones.

I am supposed to be the caregiver. I am supposed to be the one who notices, the one who guides children through their conflicted feelings. But here she is – a toddler – noticing my discontent, offering me something I needed, inviting me back into our shared experience. She notices me, and empathizes with my struggle. My heart breaks open, with gratitude and humility. The mood of my day is redeemed by the simple, beautiful gesture from a child, offering me a stick.

the gift

CHAPTER 4

stuck

He has a knack for choosing the trickier paths: the rugged trails that pass over logs, the ones that require us to cross icy streams and trudge through dense brush. Our regular trips to this place have made him a master of the landscape. When he stumbles, he gets right up; when he staggers, he grabs onto a nearby tree for balance. He knows how to move his body well in response to the obstacles he encounters in the forest. He invites challenges and is fueled by risk, so it comes as no surprise when he plows ahead of me today. He is in search of his next big adventure.

The forest welcomed an early winter snowfall overnight, and our familiar footpaths have been hidden from sight. Mounds of snow weigh down tree branches, so they bend and droop as they wait to dump their heavy burden on the head of the next passerby. The snow is deep and clings to our boot soles, which makes walking cumbersome. None of this stops him, though: he forges ahead confidently, grappling his way across uneven terrain through snow up well past his knees. He is going somewhere, guided by a plan known only to him, and as always, I am curious to find out what might be in store!

There are definitely simpler routes that one could take than the one he has chosen to lead us along. He choreographs an impressive dance through the trees that leads us forward: long strides, side steps, foot shuffles, belly flops, loop-de-loops and straightaways. Our tracks leave chaotic patterns in the snow; it would be difficult for a follower to decipher our exact route.

I notice a sort of clearing straight ahead – an easier place to walk, free from the burden of snow-draped overhanging branches and hidden vines and roots. I breathe a little easier as he leads us straight towards this spot. It will be a welcome break for some of the others, who are not so keen for this kind of physical challenge. My relief is short-lived however, when, without warning, he stumbles sideways and collapses gracelessly in the powdery snow. And there he stays, sprawled out, motionless, dusted with snow from head to toe. Fearing injury, I move towards him quickly, but then I pause. Was this part of his plan? Then I see it: that twinkle in his eyes that confirms my suspicion. He looks back at his friends, who have stopped to look at some animal tracks. The brief moment of calm is shattered by his one solitary shriek:

"Help! I'm stuck!"

The forest erupts! The children clamber through the snow, hurrying towards their friend in need. Messages of impending rescue echo through the treetops: "Hang on, buddy! We'll save you!" The children arrive at the scene in a flash, and swarm around him. They begin to push, pull, and nudge him, working with one another, working against one another, trying to get him unstuck. This is serious work and I dare not interfere.

This is their rescue mission and they have it under control; if they truly need my assistance, they will call on me.

I stay close and continue to watch, fully prepared to step in on a moment's notice. But I'm not needed. He scrambles to his feet, offers a quick, "Thanks, guys" to his rescuers, and darts past us to reclaim his lead position.

This is definitely the beginning of something new; he has carried a game that he invented in the classroom into the forest. In our classroom a few weeks ago, he buried himself under pillows, blankets, and baskets, and then cried out for the other children to help him. His buddies rushed to his aid to 'save' him. They took turns rotating through the roles of the rescuer and the rescued, in this game steeped in drama. When they were 'stuck', they brought a pang of desperation to their cries for help. When they were rescuers, they puffed out their chests and their voices became more gritty and tense. As I watched this game unfold in the classroom, I was struck by his ability to draw others into his playful world. Today, his leadership accompanies him to the forest, where the game takes on new life.

Here among the trees, the game looks a little different. The children carefully wedge themselves between trees, they intentionally plunge into the deep snow and hidden brambles, they deliberately tangle themselves in the long grass. Their "frantic" pleas for help – laced with comedic shrieks and giggles – are cast out on the wind: "Help! I'm stuck!" And the response is immediate: the other children rush to the rescue, united in their effort to free their stuck pal. Then, when the rescue is complete, the scene resets into a new configuration of carefully-contorted bodies and joyful screeches. This playful game of 'stuck' – with all the dramatics it packs – unites the group as they take turns rescuing one another.

Even through all of this excitement, we continue to move through the forest, only now the focus has shifted.

The drama of getting stuck and rescued has inspired bravery, creativity, camaraderie, and chatter.

My attention fixes on their escapades, but I intentionally stay on the periphery. All the players seem to understand the rules of the game, which are essentially the same rules that the children follow in the classroom. Everyone has a role and no one is left out. At times, I am even invited to play along!

At one point, I break my focus from the game and realize we have travelled deep into the woods. I quickly bring everyone together so we can switch gears and start our journey back to the school. Continuing to serve as the day's leader, he hurries to the front of the line and starts to carve his way out of the forest. He zigs and zags his way through the brush, weaving among prickly bushes and thorn trees. Again, this is not the most ideal path, but he is determined to lead us out on his own terms and on a path of his choosing. He is confident and he keeps a steady stride, even as his friends start to falter. The children are tired and hungry now, weighed down by soggy snow pants and rapidly diminishing spirits. We have experienced challenging walks through the forest before, but the physical nature of today's game seems to have drained everyone's energy. The children are ready to be out of the woods.

Sensing the drastic shift in mood, I call on the group to pause for a rest, to gather our strength so we can make it through the last small tract of forest growth. I can see the path just through the stands of trees. We are SO close! I try to rally our collective spirits with words of encouragement: *"We're almost there! Just a few more steps! Just through those trees!"* My words seem to bolster them, if only slightly. In the spirit of true camaraderie, we decide that for the rest of our trek through the forest, we will support one another as we move slowly together.

There are just a dozen yards of tall grass that separate us from the paved path that will lead us back to the school. I start to wade through the grass, but immediately stop in my tracks. The sound of cracking ice beneath me forces my retreat.

Oh, no.

I quickly try another route, but with even the slightest pressure, my boots sink into ankle deep, murky slush. We are so close to where we need to be, but there is no simple way to get there! How am I going to tell the group?

How am I going to tell them that we are really, legitimately, authentically stuck?

I muster the courage to face the group. I explain our predicament, and declare that our only option is to go back into the forest to find another path out. When I describe this plan, whimpers escalate to full-blown tears and cries for mommies and daddies.

I feel as though I have failed the children, though we are not in any harm.

I ought to have considered the deep snow and how it might impact our ability to move swiftly. I ought to have considered the possibility of ice, knowing that the area adjacent to the forest always floods. I ought to have been better prepared to support these children, I think to myself. I feel that my missed steps led us to this juncture.

I take a breath to steady myself, and look at the children. At this point, everyone is sobbing, *except for him*. He is calm and steady, listening carefully to every word I say. He huddles together with his friends and looks into the forest behind him. He studies the trees that line the edge of the forest, almost as if he is scouting out a new route. He is so quiet, so focused. He is planning something.

I try once again to deliver a message of positivity. "We can do this, guys! We are so close! We've got this." But I feel as though my words of encouragement are no longer helpful. I am certain that I have ruined all future forest experiences for these children. They will never want to visit this place again! Up to this point, the idea of being stuck had been quite playful. They had the power to make the rules. They experimented with different roles and scenarios. They looked out for each other. Now, the game was over, and their sense of control was gone with it. I worry how this experience might change the way they approach challenges in the forest in the future, and I worry that our escapades today might scare them away from this type of adventure. And I worry about the stories they might share with their families. I already feel as though I have disappointed the children, and I'm embarrassed at the thought of telling the families.

It troubles me that they might think less of me, that they might lose trust in me.

I desperately want a happy ending to this adventure story!

We start to make our way back to the edge of the forest, the children teary-eyed and sniffling, holding tight to my promise that together, we would take it slow. As we enter the forest again, he sprints to the front of the line and takes his place beside me. Part of me thinks, "Oh, no! He's going to lead us through the brambles again! I don't think the kids can handle that! In fact, I don't know if I can handle that!" But his energy seems to carry the group. He seems to have the capacity to confront their fears and hesitations with strength, confidence and a jovial spirit. I let him take the lead, ready to rein him in if he begins to take us off course.

"Come on, guys! This way!"

"Follow me!"

Then, three simple words manage to spur his friends on more than my words of comfort and reassurance had done:

"It's an adventure!"

Oh, my heart! How can it be that he knows exactly what the group needs to hear at exactly the moment they need to hear it?

It's an adventure! His proclamation instantly resets the tone of the group. I feel the tension lift with each step we take. Gradually, the chatter returns, then the giggles, followed by delighted shrieks that bounce off the trees. The pace quickens, and at last our destination is in our sight. He leads us out of the forest – again – and stands on the paved path, enthusiastically greeting his friends as they step onto this familiar and welcome pavement. The group's energy has come full circle now: how quickly the drama of a few moments ago seems forgotten!

As I watch these last few minutes unfold, I notice over and over again how his peers look at him. I see how much they trust and admire him. I see how they respond to his calls to action, first in the forest game and again when we were stuck. Their relationship with him runs deep. I admire the way that he carries himself in the forest. He is confident, yet cautious. He is observant, aware.

At any moment, I could have jumped in and taken charge. I could have led the group down an easier path; I could have insisted that we stay on our familiar course through the forest. But then, we wouldn't have had this beautiful story of being stuck, first playfully and then literally – and I wouldn't have had this opportunity to learn about his responsiveness to his peers. When I think back on this day, my heartbreak does not exist in the tears and fears of a group of cold, tired, hungry toddlers stuck at the edge of a forest.

Instead, the heartbreak lives in that tender moment when one child sensed that his peers needed him and he responded in a way that illuminated the value of relationship.

When he rallied the children's spirits and encouraged them to carry on, my heart split wide open. His sensitivities towards his peers moved me because he was able to offer them exactly what they needed when I couldn't.

> *Today in the forest, I learned about trust. I witnessed a group of children trust their friend as he playfully led them through the forest.*

I put my trust in him, too, in his capacity to lead the group through a challenging situation. I experienced the feeling of trust slipping away when we encountered the ice and were forced to retreat; we doubted one another and I doubted myself. I feared that the children, and their families, would lose confidence in me as an educator. Was I acting irresponsibly when I led them through the forest, knowing that the weather was unfavorable? Was I too focused on what I was trying to get from the day's experiences for myself, that I disregarded the needs and feelings of the children? Or was I simply trying to offer the children the fullest, richest, most memorable experience in nature, so they could have memories to reflect back on one day? I knew these families well, and I knew the children were strong and capable of facing challenge. Trust was the foundation of this day's adventure: trust in ourselves, trust in each other. In my heart, I knew the families trusted me and would support the decisions I made. In my heart, I knew the children trusted me, too.

He led us in, deep into our beloved forest space. He led us into joyful theatrics with his deep swan dives into the snow and his dramatic capers. He led us into challenge and risk by choosing tricky, haphazard routes. He led us into a space where emotions ran high, into a place where we felt defeated, frustrated, afraid.

Then he led us out.

With the bravery and confidence that was so needed in that moment, he led us out to our familiar path. With encouraging words and an undaunted spirit, he led us out to a place where we were reunited with the laughter and joyful calls that make our visits to the forest so special. He led us out to a place where we could look back and see this forest experience as the grand adventure it was destined to be. And he led me to consider my own actions and decisions as an educator, as well as my own fears and feelings. I am not alone in the power to make decisions; I am not alone in the capacity to lead.

stuck

CHAPTER 5

snow monkeys

It is a beautiful day for a walk in the forest. The storm overnight brought a welcome gift of snow, and lots of it! Deep, pillowy mounds blanket the landscape and our world sparkles as if it has been dusted with diamonds. The air is still; no breeze disrupts the snow. The forest is pristine, silent, untouched.

Where I stand at the edge of the field that separates us from the forest, the snow is more than knee deep for me, and I wonder how the little ones will manage to wade through it at all. It is light and feathery, though, and after a few steps, I realize that walking through it takes no effort at all. So we begin our journey across the field to the path that skirts the forest edge. The familiar neighbourhood noises – the steady stream of traffic at the roundabout, the constant chatter of the school children in their playground – are muffled this morning, hushed to mere whispers by the snow. The snowfall has created a quiet, untouched world – and we are ready to explore it.

Tranquility is suddenly disrupted as the children stampede through the knee-deep snow, etching a chaotic path that goes this way and that.

The effortlessness of their movement startles me, considering the volume of the snow.

But the snow is alluring today, and calls us to touch, to sprawl, to cast our bodies through it. We flop on our backs; the snow is so light that it billows into the air like puffs of smoke when our bodies make contact. The laughter and playful shrieks, though muted by the snow, are no less exuberant. As we move deeper into the forest, we leave deep ruts on the trail behind us, and messy piles of displaced snow frame the edges of our footpath. We've pushed decaying leaf matter from the forest floor onto the tops of snow heaps. Looking back through the forest, our presence in this space is so obvious!

I look ahead, and see a single tree still holding onto its brittle autumn foliage. The curled and muted auburn leaves stand out against our pristine white surroundings. We head towards the tree for a closer look. The snow clings to the leaves, and coats each one with a dense smear of snow, like frosting. I try to resist, but I can't: I reach out and gently tug on one leaf, sending the snow cascading down, covering the tops of the toddlers' heads. Gasps and giggles erupt!

Further along, we pause to admire a collection of thick, stalky vines that encircle a stand of trees. These vines – we know them as 'monkey vines' – twist and twine from their roots under the snow all the way up to the treetops. The monkey vines are one of our favourite things to explore in the forest; they are sturdy enough to hang on, bounce on, swing on. But we have to really look for them today; the snow has almost hidden them from sight. Eventually, we spot a beautiful arch of thick vines, so completely covered in snow that they are almost camouflaged against the wintery backdrop. One by one, we crouch down low to pass underneath the arch, trying hard not to disturb the flakes.

I notice that one of the children is falling back from the group, so I pause at the arch to wait for him. He seems completely mesmerized by the snow, consumed by the sparkle. He shuffles along happily, his legs carving deep trenches in the snow, trenches that quickly fill in as he takes his next step. He finally makes it to the arch of vines. As he crouches down low to pass underneath, his coat gets snagged! Piles of shimmering snow fall from the arch and cascade down all around him. Shocked by what has just happened, he freezes in place, eyes wide and mouth agape. He notices the sparkly snow covering his coat and mitts. He looks up to me, in astonishment.

"Snow... monkeys," he whispers.

Part of me wants to point out the obvious, that the snow fell because of the tug of his snagged jacket on the branch. But I pause, noticing the twinkle in his eyes, a glimmer that stokes my curiosities.

What if there is another story here, a tale just as magical and mysterious as the day's snow?

What would it be like to follow his version of the story instead of my own? What is the harm in watching his narrative unfold?

So I lean in and listen.

As the snow continues to sprinkle down from the arch, he shifts his gaze upward, presumably hoping to catch a glimpse of the mythical creatures who sent the snow down on us. I look up into the arch with him. And there we stand, under the vines, watching and waiting for the snow monkeys to show themselves. He whispers again, "Snow monkeys!"

This is what I love about spending my days with toddlers: they see the world as a magical place, full of possibilities, full of stories.

Spending my days with little ones offers me a chance to celebrate all that is wondrous.

This child's invitation to sidestep reality made my heart sing. It was a true, heartfelt invitation: to play, to be light in spirit, to be drenched in imagination.

He and I stand together under the arch, searching in silence, waiting, hoping to catch a glimpse of our snow-dumping culprits. My mind starts to piece together an image of a snow monkey. I imagine fluffy, wispy hair, the kind of hair that flutters in the wind. I presume that a snow monkey is mischievous, prone to trickery and sneaky snow attacks, antics triggered by the onslaught of our muffled shrieks and disruptive foot stomps through its forest home.

As my toddler companion scans the treetops, I wonder if he has conjured up his own image of a snow monkey. He must have an idea of what he is looking for as he studies the forest canopy. What clues does he see that allude to the presence of a snow monkey? What does he notice that I don't? What does he hear, or sense? I want to be present in this place of possibilities. I want to be present in a place where "snow monkeys" exist, magical and mysterious, instead of dismissing the fallen snow as a simple act of human interference.

In the forest, crouched under that snow arch, the child next to me looks up at me with wide eyes. As he scans the forest canopy for the snow monkeys that are responsible for the disturbance, I know that his search will not turn up any culprits.

But with a twinkle and a smile, I respond.

"Yes," I say. "Snow monkeys."

snow monkeys

CHAPTER 6

snail encounter

Spring.

The days early in the season bring a sensory awakening like no other! Each day, the sun rises a little earlier and sets to work warming the earth. The ground, frozen solid just weeks ago, is now soft and pliable under our feet. Runoff from the spring thaw overwhelms the shallow ditches on either side of the path. The colour palette of the landscape makes a noticeable shift, from static browns and greys to vibrant hues of green, buttery yellow, crisp white. Birdsongs saturate the air. Insects parade along the paths and sidewalks, through the grass, and up the long, brown stalks of last season's wildflowers. There are conflicting smells around us: the mustiness of decaying leaf matter, the sweet, herbal aroma of new grasses and blossoms. Spring brings with it a sense of liveliness and with so much around us to take in, we waste no time getting started.

As we begin our walk, we exchange remarks about the dampness in the air and the fresh dirt smell that comes as a result of the early morning rain. The grass is slick and slippery this morning, which tests our balance with each step we take. Pressure from our steps forces mud to seep up through the clumps of grass, creating a sucking noise that alerts us to look down. A heavy ground fog rises up from under our feet as the sun labours to warm the soil. Robust chatter, cheerful laughter and excited squeals add more layers to the day as we move across the field.

We talk as we walk.

We anticipate. What might we encounter? What might grab our attention and lure us in closer?

snail encounter

In the span of a few short steps, we declare our hopes and expectations for the day's journey. Someone mentions the possibility of seeing worms: we know from past experiences that rain drives the worms up to the surface. This ignites a fire in us: we have our plan!

We quicken our pace across the grassy field and, in no time, we arrive at the paved path that skirts the forest. With our sights set on finding worms, our eyes train downward onto the familiar path. We spot a bunch of worms wriggling frantically across the harsh concrete terrain, seeking cover from the earthshakes that our walking causes. We kneel to get a closer look at these admirable wrigglers and watch as they make their way towards the edge of the path. For us adults, this worm sighting is familiar. We have all sidestepped around worms on rainy mornings; we have all rescued a worm or two from a puddle or potential foot stomp. But we kneel down with the children anyway, recognizing this as a compelling encounter for them, and appreciating the opportunity to slow our pace.

Our quiet study is interrupted by a message shouted from a preschool group on the path ahead of us: they have discovered snails, thousands of snails! We abandon the worms and move towards the snails.

A few yards down the path, we notice a few snails moving across the walkway. We slow down to take a closer look, and then we realize that there are snails everywhere!

Snails are suctioned to stalks of wildflowers that line the path; they cling to the undersides of tender foliage. Some snails are crawling over twigs and pebbles; other snails are still, huddled in clusters. All sizes and colours are represented, and while a few snails stay concealed safely in the confines of their shells, others bravely expose their bodies to us. Standing in a close group at the edge of the swath of snails, we watch as they glide ever so slowly across the path, leaving traces of their journey in the form of shimmering slime trails. Fascinated by these tiny creatures, we start to spread out across the path so we can each admire the snails in our own ways. Some of the children point out "mommy snails" and "baby snails" while others search for the biggest, stripiest snails they can find. My co-educator and I step to the opposite side of the path and allow ourselves to get swallowed up in this beautifully tranquil moment. Then it happens.

Crunch. Crunch. Crunch.

The sound is barely audible at first, but distinct enough for us to notice. It is not unlike the sound of twigs snapping or the grinding of fine gravel underfoot. We hear the grittiness, the friction, the harshness. As children move about the path to study the snails, they create a symphony of *crunches*. It takes us adults a minute to realize what is happening. What is making this sound? Then it hits us.

Oh no!

snail encounter

The snails.

Crunch. Crunch. Crunch.

The adults in the group exchange glances, horrified, frozen in place. Waves of guilt wash over us.

What do we do?

What have we done?

Crunch.

Each step that the children take is an auditory assault that elongates the torturous onomatopoeia.

Crunch.

A tragic clash of the human and more than human worlds. Personally, I feel sick, confronted with such a blatant reminder that our actions have consequences, that my thoughtless, careless steps were a murderous gait. I feel shattered, like the snails we leave in our tracks.

Crunch. CRUNCH. C-R-U-N-C-H!

The adults congregate and discuss our potential next steps. Do we backtrack and try another route or do we forge ahead? We could walk on the grass: surely the snails are there too, but at least we won't hear the crunching. Does that make it okay? We could step off the path and choose an alternate route; perhaps taking the sidewalk adjacent to the school is a viable option today. But there could well be snails on the sidewalk, too. We could continue on our current trajectory, hoping that this cluster of snails is an isolated occurrence on the path. But what if it isn't? What if the entire path offers us more of the same experience? Can we tolerate more of this? We struggle with our choices, since no one option seems better than the rest. Eventually – painfully – we decide to continue along the path.

Decision made, we brace ourselves for what's to come, but before we can move, a joyous cacophony arises from across the path. The children are talking to the snails! "Hello, baby snail," I hear them say. "Where's your mommy?" "I like your stripes!" "Where are you going?" "Is that flower your house?"

The children are oblivious to our anguish, unaware of the angst experienced by us adults.

Their relentless enthusiasm for the snails jolts us out of our story of death and grief, and challenges us to see their story of this encounter with the snails, a story of innocence, curiosity, amazement and the awe of a new discovery. We delicately, wincingly make our way across to join them on the sunnier side of the path, and begin to listen closely to *their* story.

Crouched along the edge of the path, the children watch as the snails move into the grass, towards the wildflowers. The children inch towards the flowers, too, getting so close that their noses almost touch the dewy petals and leaves. They study the snails intimately, their gazes fixed on their subjects as they watch the scene unfold before them. They don't know what to expect. Will the snails jump? Will they make a sound? Will they move fast or slow? The children stare at these intriguing beings. Mesmerized. Captivated. Present to the life all around us, young and old, big and small. Human and more than human.

The scene is uncomplicatedly beautiful and innocent, so different from the horrifying devastation we adults had recognized just a few steps away. The children inhabit a very different story than our adult story.

They didn't hear the crunch.

They don't feel our burden of awareness.

Their bodies aren't paralyzed by guilt and their hearts don't ache.

They didn't see what we saw and they don't feel what we feel. And at first we didn't see the snail encounter through their eyes, either. But now we do.

My heart melts. Though I cannot dismiss the brutal crunching of the snails under my heavy feet, the children remind me to see more than that. This was a moment of heartbreak for me: the toddlers, with their robust enthusiasm, invited me to cross the path into their experience, to witness the liveliness, the joy, the innocence of their snail encounter. This was such a contradiction of my experience. The children's experience did not take away the discomfort I felt knowing that my actions had dire consequences for the snails. But being a witness to the children's story reminded me that different stories emerge from the same moment. It reminded me that I can orient my presence in a moment with curiosity, ready to listen, to feel deeply, to consider other stories.

Heartbreak positioned me to experience the joy and beauty of the children's story

just as deeply as I felt the tension and devastation an arm's reach away. It reminded me of the value of bringing awareness to the multiple stories at play in every experience, and how this awareness can shift my work as an educator.

snail encounter

CHAPTER 7

broken

From the playground we hear it: the familiar groans and rumblings of the massive earth movers at work. Our neighbourhood is rapidly expanding and as a result we are accustomed to construction activity everywhere we look. We tolerate the near-constant auditory assault of heavy machinery, and the shrill "BEEP...BEEP...BEEP" of their reversing alarms. This has been our daily experience since our school opened a few years ago, and despite construction seemingly near completion, the chaos and noise has yet to subside.

In the early days, it was truly a thrill: the toddlers exclaimed at the sight of an excavator

and enthusiastically mimicked the beeps and grumbles it spewed. Many of our outings walked us past active construction sites where we could witness the commotion at close range. The group squealed with delight at the sound of those beeps! Over time, however, the scene has become ordinary, perhaps even predictable. The excitement has diminished. Now, the sight of a dump truck barely causes a stir and the sounds that once sparked so much enthusiasm don't even register. Construction – and living and learning at the epicentre of a construction zone – has become our new normal.

This morning, when we exit the playground and head towards the forest, there is a wild enthusiasm in the group. Finally, after a string of wet and dreary days, we have a bit of sunshine to accompany us on our walk! The children's excited calls and laughter braid through their repeated pleas for everyone to hurry.

As we make our way down the path, our attention shifts to the familiar noises of construction. Admittedly, the sounds are no longer met with the same enthusiasm and reverence they once were, but we still acknowledge their presence in our space.

"I hear a digger!"

"I think it's backin' up!"

"Beep...Beep...Beep..."

Something is striking about today, though. The sounds are coming from a different place, not from the usual spot at the end of the new cul-de-sac. It seems much closer to us, which is confusing, since all the construction projects adjacent to our school are complete. More cautiously now, we continue to move down the path.

Louder and louder, step by step. As we round the corner, the smell of freshly turned soil collides in sharp contrast with the pungent, smoky sweetness of diesel fumes. And there it is, the source of those familiar sounds: an entire crew lined up in procession along the edge of the paved walking trail. The machines are poised for action, their exhausts chugging, their drivers congregating, presumably confirming their plan of action. I am stunned. Construction of the path has been completed for some time now. What are they doing here?

We pause to decide the best route into the forest so we can steer clear of the excavators. I feel as though I am only half listening to our conversation, though, because I am so distracted by the frenzy at the forest edge. Flaming orange tape knots itself around spindly tree trunks, and the ends of it flap wildly in the breeze.

A larger tree at the entrance has been emblazoned with an oversized 'X' tattoo on its bark. The noise is loud now, and I can feel the vibrations course through my body. It is overwhelming and uncomfortable to be here. Then it hits me: I realize what they are doing here.

THE FOREST!

Engines roar and the machines begin to move.

We are frozen in our tracks, in utter disbelief of what we are witnessing.

Engines and alarms. Steel scraping on stone. Crunching and crushing, tree limbs snapping under pressure. The excavators relentlessly tear away at our little forest, aggressively plucking mature root systems from the soil. Bulldozers push, the landscape resists, but ultimately the forest meets defeat.

It is all over in a matter of minutes; the machines retreat. Their work for the day done, the filthy caravan moves on. All is quiet again. It is almost as if they were never there, but the devastation they have left in their wake testifies to their brutal presence. The landscape of our little forest is changed forever.

We slowly walk towards the site, and my heart sinks.

> *I see where the machines have savagely knocked down the trees. I see where the earth has been turned over on itself, mounding and exposing fractured roots, severing their lifelines.*

I blink back tears. This is a small-scale project, but it is devastating nonetheless. I look at the children, recalling the spirit and vibrancy I felt radiating from them just moments ago. Now, they stand beside me at the edge of the forest and stare in at the site. Ever so slowly, we move in for a closer look. At first, no one speaks. We just stand there, shocked, nudging the overturned soil with the toes of our boots. The longer we stand there in silence, the more anxious I feel. What I see infuriates me, confuses me, saddens me. Finally, the silence breaks.

"The trees are broken."

"It fell down."

"What happened?"

And perhaps the biggest question that is on all our minds: "WHY?"

We continue to edge into the forest, uncharacteristically clumped together in a tight group. This place, so familiar to us, is now unrecognizable, maybe even a little scary. Our familiar entry point has been permanently altered, scraped down to its rocky foundation. The rugged, uneven terrain that we loved to scramble over has been levelled and smoothed and prettied up with a bucket-load of sparkly pea gravel. Mounds of upturned soil and wrecked trees frame the freshly cut, angular edges of the path. This new gateway, presumably intended to invite us in, has quite the opposite effect. No one is sure how to respond to what we see, what we feel, so we just stand there. I wait for the children to make the first move.

I want to take my cue from them because, honestly, I am not sure how to be here.

In time, they start to wander from our tight-clumped group, and I watch as they cautiously shuffle through the soil. Slowly, they begin to explore, sliding their hands into the earth in search of treasures that have been unearthed. They examine once-hidden roots, train their eyes on the suddenly homeless insects now scurrying to find shelter. And I just stand there, frozen in place, fearing the questions that might surface.

What if they ask me why? What would I say? I don't really understand it myself, so how can I possibly explain this destruction to the children? I am angry and confused... and I am hurting.

Then I see her, the youngest child in our group. She has stayed behind the pack, which is out of character for her. She is typically lively and rambunctious, but in this moment, she is almost sedate; her calm demeanor offers a sharp contrast to the turbulent scene around us. She moves slowly, and each deliberate step carries her through the clay until she is beside one of the sacrificial trees. The orange 'X' on its trunk is barely noticeable through the layers of caked-on mud and scrapped foliage. The force from the bulldozer only tore the tree partially from the ground before gravity took over and wrenched it downwards, violently snapping the trunk. The tree just hangs there now, suspended somewhere between vertical and horizontal, between living and dying, between potent and powerless. At the break, its insides are exposed, raw and jagged, vulnerable. Slowly, she stretches out her hand, reaching out with softness and delicacy. Her fingertips gently caress the bark. Her touch pulls her in even closer until her body brushes up against the tree. She drags her fingers back and forth along the bark, silently, stoically. She must sense that I am watching, and she turns and looks at me.

"Broken," she whispers, as she strokes the tree.

"Ouch," she continues, her fingertips tracing the jagged peaks at the break.

I hesitate before responding; something tells me that she is not done sharing her story with me yet. She turns and faces the tree and leans into it. With awkward determination, she stretches her body across the trunk. She turns her head to one side and presses her soft, rosy cheek against the ragged bark. As she gently drums her fingertips on the trunk, her embrace draws out one more message, directed toward the tree.

"*It's okay,*" she whispers.

She presses her fingertips to her lips, then releases a kiss onto the wind, a kiss destined for the broken tree. She lingers there for a moment, straddled across the tree, and looks out into the forest. Then she scrambles to her feet and heads off to join her friends. And I am left standing there, beside that broken tree, trying to come to terms with what I have just witnessed.

The earth movers are gone, and the damage is done. We can choose to avoid our beloved place because its scars make us feel sad or angry or guilty, or we can choose to remember why we love this place so much to begin with. She helped me to see our little forest differently today. I saw beyond the excavators and the broken trees and I was reminded of the deep love and admiration that we hold for this place. I was reminded of its sensitivities, of its fragility. For us, its beauty goes beyond the physical aesthetic of mature trees and lush undergrowth, and rests in the footfalls and muddy fingertips of our shared adventures there. We love this place in all its messiness and chaos.

Just like that, the landscape of our little forest changed forever, but our relationship remains as strong as ever. I saw it when she caressed the tree, whispering "Broken." I saw it in her warm embrace with the fallen tree and in the gentle kiss she released on the wind.

Just like that,

her simple words and heartfelt gesture turned a troubling moment into the most magnificent encounter.

And just like that, 'broken' became beautiful.

CHAPTER 8

hush

Hush.

Don't say a word.

Let the silence speak its wisdom.

Let its whispers be my guide across the terrain.

If I listen hard enough, I can hear it.

This silence goes unnoticed when the children are here with me. It's here (it is always here!) but when the children are here with me, the silence retreats, hiding under layers of boisterous laughter, child-sized footfalls and joyful shrieks. And there it stays, until something calls on it to make itself known.

Hush.

The birds' sweet melodic songs carry through the trees, as they flit from one branch to the next, mapping a chaotic sky dance. A robin darts and dives around me, seeming to be annoyed by my presence. She flies right at me, tweeting wildly! Expecting the worst, I duck down and hide my face, but thankfully, she modifies her flight plan at the last second. All I feel is a slight disturbance in the breeze as her wingtips kiss the leaves just above my head.

A squirrel scampers to the top of the tree to delight in a feast of nuts from his cache. He scratches at the tree, trying to maintain his precarious grip on the bark. Boughs bend and sway as the squirrel leaps and clings, leaps and clings. The disturbed leaves shake wildly for just a moment before they fall silent once more. The squirrel comes to rest on a sturdy branch and starts to devour its snack. Walnut debris cascades down around me. Thud! Thud! Thud!

Just ahead of me, a family of deer postures most alertly, maintaining distance as they watch my every move.

The doe is closest to me, statuesque, holding her place as she protects her young. Then, without warning, the deer bolt, and if I hadn't been watching, I would never have known they were there. They barely make a sound as they disappear from my sight.

Hush.

As I carve my way through the forest,

I am startled by the incredible racket I produce!

Every move I make contributes to the orchestral swell that fractures the silence: the snapping recoil of the tender branch that gets snared on my pack, the obtrusive crackle of the groundcover as it succumbs to the weight of my foot, the heavy clunks and crashes of disrupted rocks as they compete to find a new resting place on the forest floor. Off to my left, I hear the stream peacefully trickling as it casts its effervescent droplets onto the wind. The water produces a calming and delicate sound, a contrast to the violent journey over rocks and forest debris that it must endure. And under my clatter and the stream's flow, under the deer's bounds and the bird songs and the squirrel's climb, the silence is always there.

Hush.

This is my first trip to the forest on my own, without the toddlers.

> *I do not come here alone today by choice, but out of necessity. I need to come back to this place, to rekindle a lost connection,*

to conjure memories of our time spent here together because I am beginning to feel disconnected. But just a few steps into the forest, I freeze. I don't want to do this. I don't want to be here without them! It's just too quiet, unnaturally quiet. Even with all the forest sounds, the silence is deafening. I feel out of place! I argue with myself: something brought me here, something inspired me to come. I plant my feet firmly on the ground and I close my eyes tight. With any luck, just standing still will trigger it all to come rushing back to me. So, with my eyes closed tight, I wait.

Hush. Don't say a word.

I can hear them!

Faintly at first, their giggles and chatter sound like a distant echo. Their sounds build slowly, and with volume comes clarity. I squeeze my eyes closed even tighter, wanting so desperately to see them. The images are fuzzy and faded at first, appearing in my mind's eye as blurry balls of energy darting among the trees. They are running, flopping, diving and crouching behind stumps and fallen logs. *A-ha!* They are playing hide-and-seek! They stay still only briefly and then they are on the move again, darting about in search of the next hiding spot. Sometimes they do not even hide at all! Rather, they flop in a clearing and giggle until one of their friends comes to 'find' them. They really don't need to be found; they are completely within sight, but that doesn't seem to matter. Slowly, the scene comes into focus. I recognize this game from our time together in the forest and it is a welcome old friend. As long as my eyes are squeezed shut tight, they are there with me, and in their company, although imagined, I no longer feel alone.

It has been a challenging time, this coronavirus pandemic, with its shutdowns and lockdowns. Our childcare centre closed with less than a day's notice and my time with the toddlers came to an abrupt halt. We didn't have a chance to say good-bye or to tie up loose ends. Everyone just hurried home. None of us knew if we would be gone for days, or weeks, or months.

Our forest adventures had become something that I looked forward to each day. When the pandemic put an end to our forest visits, I felt an incredible sense of loss. We had made so many plans, charted so many future adventures together, and now I felt bereft, unsure whether our plans would ever come to fruition. I missed the children. I missed the way we moved through the forest, I missed the way their hands caressed the tree bark and how their feet stampeded through the muck.

> *So I went to the forest to seek solace; to reacquaint myself with the memories we had made there.*

And through those memories, I hoped to satisfy my longing to be with the children, and with the forest itself.

Hush.

A sudden rustling in the treetops startles me back to my solitary presence in the forest. I take a moment to gather my wits, and perhaps even mourn a little for that fleeting game of hide-and-seek. Standing there on my own, I am once again struck by the silence. The forest chatter seems muted now, an asynchronous hum that sharply contradicts the wild darting and weaving of the forest inhabitants. Amidst the visual chaos, I look up, just in time to see her as she swoops down from her roost. She pitches and rolls effortlessly, navigating her way through the tops of trees. She rests on a branch directly in front of me and flaps her wings, shaking her flight feathers into place. Then, fully coiffed, she rotates her head and fixes her gaze down on me. Our eyes lock.

Great Horned Owl.

This familiar friend often escorts me and the little ones on our forest adventures. She motivates us to move swiftly through the forest and challenges us to keep her in our sight. Seeing her today comforts me as I struggle with the tension of being in the forest on my own; she evokes the time I've shared here with the children. Her presence here with me in this moment is a gift.

Hush.

Don't say a word.

I stare at this majestic aviator, mesmerized by her golden eyes, taken aback by her staggering beauty. Eyes locked, both of us motionless, time seems to stand still. Eventually, I begin to move towards her, slowly, gingerly, and she watches every move. I am awkward and graceless as I stomp and clod my way through the brush. *"Am I always this noisy?"* I wonder. A stick snaps under my foot and the shock of it shatters my gaze. I only look down for a second, but when I look up again, she is gone.

I stop in my tracks and try to regain my composure. I pivot around to try to find her. I search hard (perhaps too hard), scanning each tree from the ground up. At one point, I almost give up, convinced that she has moved on without me, but then I look up into the trees one more time.

And there she is, in plain sight, waiting for me to see her again.

Hush.

The sight of her in those trees delights me! "Hello, old friend," I say, offering an acknowledgement of our long relationship. Our eyes lock again, and more quickly and sturdily than before, I start to move towards her. She reciprocates by taking flight, swooping through the trees without a sound, until she lands on a bare branch once more.

It is like a game for us now, not unlike that game of hide-and-seek I'd pictured in my mind's eye. I am eager to play, and she has my full attention. I await her next move. I plant my feet firmly and lock eyes with her. It is imperative that I have laser focus here; she seems to know the precise moment when I am distracted and takes that opportunity to fly off to her next treetop perch. She is an expert at this game! The way she moves reminds me of the way the little ones move in the forest. Like the Owl, the children dart from place to place; they anticipate my countermoves, and lead me deeper into the forest and into our shared encounters.

The owl, like the children in the forest, captures my attention and inspires me to play along.

hush

So I follow her diligently, past a stream, through some muck and across a downed barbed wire fence. I try hard to keep up with her, but she is just too fast! Finally, I stop to watch her as she slips between the trees that border the forest and continues to fly out of sight.

So long, friend. See you again soon.

Hush.

I slump down on a fallen log, sad to see my winged companion go. And I miss the children desperately. My heart aches for the days when we tromped through the forest together, following our companion, the owl, from one perch to the next. I long to hear the children's laughter again, even just for a moment. But instead, the deafening silence rebounds, more palpable than ever. It sits on me heavily, uncomfortably, posturing itself as a stern reminder that I am alone.

I look around to orient myself. This place is so familiar to me! With renewed intrigue, I study the landscape. To my left, there is the tree that housed last year's owl nest high up in the canopy. We gathered under that tree on many occasions, waiting to catch a glimpse of one of the owlets. The nest has been abandoned now, broken down and exhausted of all usefulness as a home for any creature. But even in its dilapidated state, it's still one of our favourite forest landmarks. Just off in the distance over my right shoulder, I see the "sideways tree" and I remember those fearless toddlers bravely scrambling up the steep incline. Their determination was something to admire! And straight ahead, I notice the slightest gap in the foliage, a gap that frames a discrete path that leads directly to the place where we all once got stuck. I recall that challenging walk, when we were tripped up by brambles, demoralized by dropping temperatures and rising frustrations. It was quite the adventure, though, and it laid the groundwork for so many tales of bravery!

I blink, and tears fill my eyes. It seems my friend, the Owl, led me right to this place made of memories, exactly where I needed to be. As I sit in the forest, I think about all of the stories that the children and I crafted together here. I feel my loneliness slip away, and my heart is nestled in nostalgia, flooded with happy stories, memories of shared moments, and laughter and challenge and triumph.

Hush.

I can hear them again!

I hear them calling out to the owl, spurring on a game of hide-and-seek.

I hear their feet slip and slide against the slick, moss-covered base of the "sideways tree."

hush

I hear the whimpers from the little ones and the exhausted cries for mommy and daddy from the place where we got stuck in the forest on that cold, wet day.

I hear them all around me and I no longer feel alone.

> *We are part of the same stories, tales that emerged from time spent together among tall trees and brambles,*

along rain-soaked paths on dreary days, in mud puddles and snow drifts.

They are here with me!

Through the silence. In solitude.

They are here, with me.

Hush.

My mind is quiet, free from the compulsion to assess and analyze every action, liberated from worry and an overwhelming sense of loss. My mind is quiet and my heart breaks open once more. I am reminded of the joy of living life whole-heartedly, with steadfast presence and in absolute awe of my young companions. This is who I choose to be: an educator who looks beyond the measured and the analytical, one who can be still and quiet and vulnerable and fully human. I am an educator who moves through my days with children with my heart primed to burst wide open at any moment.

Hush.

hush

© London Bridge Child Care Services

about the author

Shelley is an Early Years Educator and Pedagogical Leader. She holds a BA(Hons) in History from Western University as well as a Diploma in Early Childhood Education from Fanshawe College. Shelley's career in early years settings spans over 28 years. When she's not in the forest with a group of children, Shelley is planning her next big Canadian road trip with her sister and her dogs. Shelley resides in London, Ontario, Canada.

coda

There was something about Aleena that has always stayed with me, beyond our farewell at the preschool classroom door, and even beyond that phone call from her mom.

Aleena moved through life guided by her heart. She called my attention to beautiful moments that might have otherwise gone unnoticed. She reminded me to be fully present and open to experiencing life whole-heartedly.

After Aleena's death I spent months trying to write a story that would both honour her life and celebrate her liveliness. Memories of our time spent together always stayed close to my heart, and it was those memories that began to influence how I saw other stories unfold. I tried to write Aleena's story so many times, but the right words just wouldn't come to me.

So, I started to write stories about experiences I shared with other children. I dove deep into heartbreak, and whole-heartedness, and nostalgia, and humanness. Suddenly, Aleena's story-the one I had longed to write for such a long time- began to emerge. And before I knew it, Aleena's story became the anchor for this collection of stories about reimagining heartbreak.

I shared the original manuscript with Aleena's mom, Amber, and I anxiously awaited her response. On the anniversary of Aleena's death, I received this message:

"I waited until today to read your manuscript. It was the perfect gift for me today. I loved every chapter. It truly made me realize I need to let go of some of my anger and enjoy the little things in life. You explained seeing life through the eyes of a child so perfectly and it's beautiful." –Amber

With gratitude always, for what Aleena taught me.

Shelley

coda

STUDY GUIDE |

From Reading to Thinking:
A Protocol for Reflection and Learning

In the Foreword, we suggested one theme song for this book. Here's another candidate, by troubadour Tom Hunter[1]:

> *This world is changing so fast we can't*
> *see what's coming before it arrives.*
>
> *To think passing tests will get our kids ready*
> *is a gamble we play with their lives.*
>
> *How can we prepare our children*
> *for a world we cannot yet see?*
>
> *I say we work hard so they can*
> *become as human as they can be.*

The stories in *Reimagining Heartbreak* are testaments to Shelley's commitment to be as human as she can be, standing in wholehearted witness to the children, who are as human as they can be.

---

1) *As Human as They Can Be Tribute*, The Song Growing Company, 2008.

Shelley is determined to "look beyond the analytical side of learning ... [and] formal assessments and see children for the whole-hearted humans that they are." And to do that, she reclaims whole-heartedness for herself: "The educator part of me had forgotten the human part of me, the part that draws me in close to experiences and holds me there. ...I have decided to tell stories about the beautiful moments that break open my heart. When I connect to my own heart in this way, I become more aware of the children's hearts."

By connecting to our own hearts, we tune ourselves to children's hearts. That is surely what it means to "work hard so that [children] can become as human as they can be."

This is challenging work. And it's our primary work: to show up for life, with our hearts as open as we can crack them. This sounds simple, perhaps foolishly so. But it is the most rigorous work we can do. It asks that we show up all the way in our days with children, not hovering on the surface with developmental checklists and academic goals, but seeking the human heart of each moment we share with children, and then carrying the stories of those moments into the community. Shelley reminds us that:

> Whole-heartedness ... serves as a portal to experiencing life and living, with robust attention and commitment to being present ... more receptive, more responsive to the spirit of the moment.

As an educator – as a human – it serves as a reminder for me to feel, to express, to reflect on those beautiful moments shared with children.

The poet W. H. Auden[2] wrote that, "in order to be a scientist, an artist, a doctor, a lawyer, or what-have-you, one has first to be a human being." Shelley puts "educator" front and center on that list: In order to be an educator, we must first be human beings, hearts wide open, with our sensitivities guiding us.

In her documentation and in this book, Shelley writes from her generous human heart. This flies in the face of how many of us were taught to write about children: to keep our hearts out of it, to "observe" children and to "document" their learning and their development. That's how Shelley used to write – before she met Aleena and felt a startling kinship with her that reminded her of who she was as a child. Shelley's stories about Aleena "captured Aleena's spirit in a genuine way," and became a source of comfort to her family after Aleena died. Aleena's life and death were the catalysts for Shelley to jettison her former approach to documentation, and to commit to writing from her heart, including herself in her writing, "describing how a child's actions affected me, how a simple encounter mattered to my heart. I used Aleena's stories as a reference

---

2) W.H. Auden, Introduction to *The Star Thrower*, by Loren Eisley. Wildwood House, 1979.

point because I saw Aleena so vividly within that writing, and I started to see myself more clearly, too."

Novelist and essayist Anne Lamott[3] says this about writing:

> In order to be a writer, you have to learn to be reverent. If not, why are you writing?
>
> Let's think of reverence as awe, as presence in and openness to the world. The alternative is that we stultify, we shut down. Think of those times when you've read prose or poetry that is presented in such a way that you have a feeling of being startled by beauty or insight, by a glimpse into someone's soul. All of a sudden everything seems to fit together or at least to have some meaning for a moment. This is our goal as writers: to help others have this sense of wonder, of seeing things anew, things that can catch us off guard, that break in on our small, bordered worlds. When this happens, everything feels more spacious.

Shelley's stories grow from reverence – from whole-hearted participation in the days she shares with children. Shelley's writing

---

[3] Anne Lamott, *Bird by Bird: Some Instructions on Writing and Life*, Pantheon Books, 1994.

offers glimpses into her soul, and into the children's souls. Her stories catch us off guard, invite a sense of wonder, of seeing children – and the natural world, and ourselves – with fresh eyes.

Consider the ways in which Shelley's stories break in on your world, challenging you to reconsider how you understand your work as an educator. Take time to revisit her stories and the notes that you took about:

- savoring hot chocolate in the snowy forest;
- following the lead of the child-as-teacher;
- receiving the gift of a walking stick;
- getting lost and found in the woods;
- encountering the antics of snow monkeys;
- witnessing the lives and deaths of snails;
- comforting wrecked trees.

As you read and reflect, allow yourself to be startled by beauty and insight, carried into a more spacious understanding of your work and of your human life. Shelley allowed these experiences to transform her, and her stories hold the potential to transform you and your work as an educator.

The Thinking Lens© protocol can be a companion to you as you revisit Shelley's stories in this light. (See the book *From Teaching to Thinking: A Pedagogy for Reimagining Our Work* for a full description of how the Thinking Lens Protocol can deepen your reflections.) We offer the questions below, built on the guideposts in the Thinking Lens, to support your study of *Reimagining Heartbreak* and to help you articulate your thinking, perhaps in writing, and then in conversation with colleagues and pedagogical companions.

Know yourself. Open your heart to this moment.
Shelley writes, "The educator part of me had forgotten the human part of me, the part that draws me in close to experiences and holds me there." How have you experienced the false separation between your work identity and your human life?

When Shelley integrates the educator part of herself with the human part of herself, she finds "a more complete version of myself, fully engaged and present," someone who "feels fully and cares relentlessly." How would you describe the more complete version of yourself?

When you find you've strayed from your intentions for who you want to be, what helps you reclaim your human heart?

Take the children's points of view.
How do you understand this declaration from Tom Stoppard: "Because children grow up, we think a child's purpose is to grow up, but a child's purpose is to be a child"?

Have you met a child who reminds you of who you were as a child? What impact did that have on you?

In Shelley's stories, we encounter the perspectives of children. Did one of these children especially lift you out of your adult way of thinking into new ways of seeing?

Do you have your own story of being startled by joy and beauty as you watched and listened to a child? Of being moved to gratitude, or to humble self-awareness?

Examine the environment.
What about the forest environment allowed both Shelley and the children to encounter new things about themselves?

How does being outside in the natural world build competency with taking risks — for children and for adults?

Are there ways in which we humans can experience kinship with the natural world if our days are primarily spent indoors or in human-made environments?

Collaborate with others to expand perspectives.
What do you understand about why some people find urban environments safer than places with more trees than buildings?

How might you and your co-workers negotiate different comfort levels with risk-taking, with being outdoors in all sorts of weather, with connecting with creatures other than humans?

How could you work with colleagues to challenge the prevailing idea that documentation should be focused on children's academic learning and developmental milestones? How could you challenge the notion that educators ought to be "neutral observers" when they write documentation stories, rather than including their own perspectives and musings in their stories?

If you and your colleagues were to work with the lyrics of Tom Hunter's song that opens this study guide, what conversations would you hope to have?

Reflect and take action.
Building on your reflections, write a statement that describes the learning that you will carry with you from *Reimagining Heartbreak*.

What will you do differently in your work, because of reading this book?

Reading a book is an investment of time and attention. To make the most of that investment, revisit sections of the book that engaged or confused you. Find study companions to help you reflect on the stories in *Reimagining Heartbreak*. Commit yourself to transform your reading from a passive experience of listening to a good story to an active engagement with thinking and questioning. Reading a book in this way becomes professional development.

We don't typically think of heartbreak as a positive experience, but Shelley shows us how we can reimagine what it means to allow our hearts to break open. She reminds us what is available to us when we live whole-heartedly, caring relentlessly. This is a tall order in a world so fraught with grief and insecurity. Shelley reminds us that living with heartbreak positions us to experience joy and beauty, tenderness and promise, alongside loss and anguish.

May you, like Shelley, choose to be an educator who looks beyond the measured and analytical, an educator guided by your sensitivities. May you recognize that you have a potent role in the stories that emerge from your days with children. May you be willing to be courageously whole-hearted and whole-heartedly courageous.

—Ann Pelo and Margie Carter
  Editors of the *Reimagining Our Work* (ROW) Collection
  Authors of *From Teaching to Thinking: A Pedagogy for Reimagining Our Work*

colophon

Paper Stock: Cover – 12pt C1S in White, BWT: 140;
Text – Inkjet Offset Eggshell in B18 Natural, BWT: 24

Finishing: Perfect bindery; soft touch lamination

Print Production: Documation in Eau Claire, WI

Typefaces: Mrs Eaves and Journal designed by Zuzana Licko (Emigre Foundry)

Interior Illustrations: Hand painted with bamboo brush and Magic Star india ink by Chad Hawthorne

Cover Credits: Adobe Stock/ Mari Ka – pine branch; kris_art – feather; Capture And Compose – tree rings; Chelmicky – torn paper